What a Winner!

Written by Teresa Heapy

Illlustrated by Jess Mikhail

C000291957

I like to do lots of things. Oh yes,
I like to win! But odd things just
keep happening to me.

I like ping pong. I whack the ball
hard with my bat. Wham!

But *this* bat wins!
What a good shot.

I like snap and whist. I have all the right cards.

But a quick crab wins!
What a big shock!

I like chess. I think hard.
I think I can do it.

But the black king wins!
What bad luck!

I like dot-to-dots. This picture might win in a contest.

But my bug shoots into the air! Whee!
I will not win.

I like shopping with Dad. I like
Alphabet Pops. You can win a free
dragon! I need one right now.

Dad is strict. I pick up the mess.
He does not let me win the dragon.
What a fuss!

I like running with Spot. I think I can whizz past him. But hang on! Wait, Spot!

13

Oh no, Spot is the winner!
When will I win? I must win one thing!

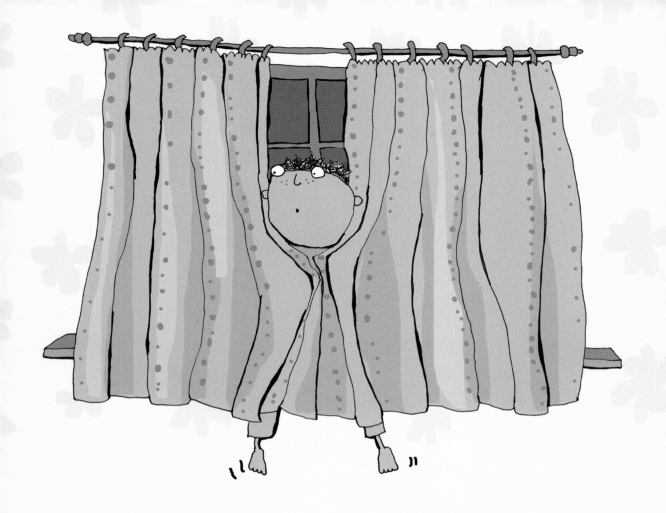

Will my pet, Dolphin, see me?
Can he find me?

No, but I find him! What a winner!